Gamble Garden

LANDSCAPE *of* OPTIMISM

Published by Elizabeth F. Gamble Garden
1431 Waverley St., Palo Alto, California 94301

Printed in the United States of America

 MIX
Paper
FSC FSC® C012561

Printed on paper stock certified by
Forest Stewardship Council®

Printed with vegetable
oil-based inks

ISBN: 978-0-692-26322-8

All proceeds from the sale of this book go to Elizabeth F. Gamble Garden
a 501 c(3) organization. Thank you for your support.

www.gamblegarden.org

Gamble Garden

LANDSCAPE *of* OPTIMISM

THE ELIZABETH F. GAMBLE GARDEN
PALO ALTO, CALIFORNIA

Susan Woodman

Foreword by Lucy Tolmach

The Elizabeth F. Gamble Garden

is dedicated to maintaining and enhancing

our historic home and garden

as an oasis of beauty and tranquility,

providing a community resource for

horticultural education, inspiration, and enjoyment.

—MISSION STATEMENT

To make a great garden,

one must have

a great idea or

a great opportunity.

—Sir George Sitwell

CONTENTS

Acknowledgments

You do your best work when you're joyful.

—Dan Kiley

You work with the best people when you get involved in a garden, and I have been enormously fortunate to collaborate with three creative, discerning, and wonderfully companionable women. A few years ago, Susan Benton, Chris Stein, Jane Stocklin, and I met to consider what kind of project might benefit Gamble Garden. We had no idea what would come from that meeting, but at the end we were exhilarated by the ease with which we agreed to create a full-length book to showcase the garden. Excited and full of resolve, the four of us entered a maze of our own making.

That first meeting was short, but everything afterwards was not. How might we best capture and present the Gamble story? What kind of book would engage and inspire people, including those outside the immediate community?

We continually re-imagined a volume with meaningful narrative, replete with color photographs. Our goal was a book that would be both smart and beautiful. We met regularly, and at least one of us showed up at Gamble with camera in hand to record events and photograph the garden throughout the seasons. Reams of ideas and trails of pixels were left on the cutting room floor.

In time, pictures and plans took shape, and I began writing and laying out pages. Susan, Chris, and Jane could always be counted on for their invaluable skills and to help keep the project true to our original concept. I am deeply appreciative of their contributions to this book and for their friendship.

Susan Woodman

Elizabeth F. Gamble Garden gratefully acknowledges
John A. and Cynthia Fry Gunn
for their support and generous underwriting of this book

With sincere appreciation for additional underwriting from
Jane and Bill Stocklin

Thanks to all the Gamble Garden friends, volunteers, and professionals who were called upon for their expertise in creating this book. Each one was extraordinarily generous.

Manuscript Readers
Frederick Baron, Kathryn Baron, Lee Benton, Jeanette Phelps,
Bill Stocklin, Lucy Tolmach, Douglas Woodman, Jane Woodman

Photographers
Susan Benton, Merrill Jensen, Joanne Koltnow, Vanessa Roach, Chris Stein,
Bill Stocklin, Jane Stocklin, John Stocklin, Douglas Woodman, Susan Woodman

Copy Editor	Graphic Layout	Botanical Editor
Hilary Hanon	Kathy Schniedwind	Lesley Peters

Liaison	Garden Guides	End Papers Artist
Jane Stocklin	Ella Ancheta & Gwen Whittier	John Haynes

Gamble Garden Board Reviewers
President	Colette Rudd
Past Presidents	Lena Dawson, Helen MacKenzie, Susann Mirabella, Judy Paris, Lonnie Zarem
Executive Director	Vanessa Roach

Foreword

The first day I set foot at 1431 Waverley Street, entering through an old rusty woven wire gate more than thirty years ago, it was at the request of members of the Garden Club of Palo Alto. As the head gardener at Filoli, they asked me for my horticultural assessment of Gamble Garden and what I thought of its potential.

It was love at first sight. I stumbled onto overgrown pea gravel paths leading towards the house and discovered the bones of Elizabeth Gamble's garden with its authentic but fading boxwood parterres, its shady enclosed garden rooms defined by formal hedges and leaning latticework fencing. I remember the beds of bearded iris in full bloom by the greenhouse, a riot of bread seed poppies naturalized along the perimeter of Embarcadero Road, and bamboo teepees loaded with fragrant sweet peas. That's when I met Seiki Noro, Miss Gamble's aging retainer. He stopped his work and, like the true gentleman he was, gave me a tour of the gardens as if they had just been planted. He explained the origin of prized specimen plants including rare flowering magnolias, and the heirloom camellia and wisteria cultivars.

My professional experience running Filoli's formal garden was the force behind my convictions in support of preserving the garden and soon landed me on Gamble's board. It was hard work creating a community horticultural center. The recipe consisted of one totally charming, almost century old historic house and a garden. Add many helping hands, a successful collaboration with the City of Palo Alto, and support from Elizabeth Gamble's family. There were generous donations and grants, new members, and unfortunately lots of meetings. As I poured over this book, what struck me most was the fact that our hopes and dreams for the place had indeed come true.

Those of us remaining from the original board of trustees now laugh at some of those heated discussions sitting around Miss Gamble's dining room table, but at the time it wasn't so funny. The City was concerned about safety and wanted the perimeter hedges removed. We had to fight that battle and won by lowering the height so security vehicles could see over the hedges and into the gardens at night, and we added lighting. The City also wanted more on-site parking. We lost that battle and the two parking lots took up precious garden space.

The environmentally friendly and permeable decomposed granite surface was a disaster, created dust storms for neighbors, and eventually had to be paved. I remember arguing in favor of needing a proper tool storage shed, which was built with funding from a generous board member. We preserved the gravel paths but reconstructing the green lattice fencing and keeping it painted the original color became a big issue. Today, the green latticework fencing is one of the most important character-defining features of the garden and adds to its integrity. All things considered, we did a great job of preserving the overall patina of the place and it was well worth the effort.

The Elizabeth F. Gamble Garden is a treasure from the past and this book exudes the confidence and optimism of its original founders and the City of Palo Alto's foresight. Today the garden is paying back, offering beauty as inspiration and endless opportunities for people of all ages. This is a story about stewardship, investing in nature, and taking big risks. This model can be applied to any community with creativity and vision. This "landscape of optimism" ensures that nature will be an enduring part of Palo Alto's future.

Lucy Tolmach
Former Director of Horticulture
Filoli, a National Trust Property
Woodside, California

Muddy Boots & Party Shoes

 Gamble Garden, as it is today, was born from an extraordinary gift that has become a public place of beauty and civic pride. At her death in 1981, at the age of ninety-two, Elizabeth Frances Gamble's garden and house became the property of the City of Palo Alto, California, a transfer she set up in her 1971 will. A lengthy civic process was soon underway to determine the best use of this gift, which came with minimal guidance and no endowment to secure its future. In 1985 the two-and-a-third acre property became the Elizabeth F. Gamble Garden, a public garden, supported by its newly formed non-profit horticultural foundation.

Miss Gamble's legacies are caring for friends and family, hospitality, and life-long giving to the community. Along with her philanthropy, she took great pleasure in sharing the garden she loved. This book recalls the garden's past and shows what it has become.

Gardening is an act of optimism. Think about what can go wrong—weather, pests, diseases, poor materials, mismanagement—and yet, gardeners carry on in spite of challenges, and by trial and error, gardens abound. Along with many who headed west in the early nineteen-hundreds, the Gamble family had high expectations in relocating to California. Once settled, they succeeded in creating a garden in a climate new to them. Seventy-five years later, the people who led the way for Gamble Garden to become the public space it is now were certainly optimistic in the face of civic hurdles and the specter of substantial restoration.

The garden today is both a reflection and a reinterpretation of its original design. Change is part of the excitement at Gamble—as it is in any garden—where on-going discoveries, new ideas, and improving practices deepen our knowledge and enjoyment.

Above all, Gamble Garden is a place for people. Along with the pleasures of garden visits, active education is paramount here, with year-round classes, programs, seasonal events, and special occasions. Like the garden, these activities are ever-changing, refreshed by creative ways for learning about and experiencing Gamble and other gardens as well.

Gamble is a source of inspiration for one's own garden. It is unusually intimate for a public garden, with a scale closer to that of a private property. The design features, plant choices, and gardening practices are well within the reach of the home gardener.

Whether the ideas in the book are revelations or re-discoveries, its aim is to be a catalyst for people everywhere to engage in the deeply satisfying personal and communal activities that are garden centered. If good fortune has not given you a Miss Gamble, much can be done in partnership with existing parks, schools, and community centers.

Having an asset like Gamble in our city is a privilege and a pleasure. The stewards of the garden are the supporters, staff, and volunteers who keep Gamble thriving. As Gamble continues to evolve, its harvests are abundant and there is much to share.

Welcome to Gamble, a garden to savor on one's own, and a place to join others for learning, working, and celebrating—a landscape of optimism. The gates are open to visitors, free of charge, every day of the year. Bring your muddy boots and your party shoes.

Susan Woodman

GAMBLE NOW
and THEN

A GARDEN LEGACY

All gardens are a form of autobiography.

—ROBERT DASH

Construction of the three-story Gamble House and Carriage House began in 1902 on land that was then outside the Palo Alto city limits. The nearest streets were still unpaved and the only other developed property in the area was the Seale Ranch. As was common at the time, the fifty-four-hundred-square-foot house was likely built from plans purchased from a catalog. Special arrangements were made to have electricity extended to what later became the 1431 Waverley Street address. Walter A. Hoff designed the formal gardens here in 1908. Today Gamble Garden is part of an expansive, verdant residential neighborhood that grew up around the property.

OPPOSITE *The Gamble House viewed from the woodland area in early spring, framed by a Saucer Magnolia (Magnolia x soulangeana), left, and a Canary Island Date Palm (Phoenix canariensis), right.*

Elizabeth Frances Gamble, granddaughter of the co-founder of Procter & Gamble, left the house and garden to the City of Palo Alto at her death in 1981. Her 1971 will stipulated that she and her brother George could live there for the remainder of their lives. George, a mining engineer, spent much of his life in Lake and Napa Counties. Later he returned to the family home where he lived with his sister until his death in 1972. Afterwards, Miss Gamble was on her own for nine years.

Beginning in 1981, Miss Gamble's gift to the city generated intense interest in the community and set off lengthy and impassioned deliberations about the future of the almost eighty-year-old property that had fallen into serious disrepair. It became the City Council's charge to determine the best use of the property from a range of proposals championed by various groups.

The Garden Club of Palo Alto had frequently been invited by Miss Gamble to visit her garden and present their flower shows at her home. With its connection to Miss Gamble and shared interest in gardening, the club's wish was for the property to be preserved and become a public horticultural center.

After much discussion and organizing, the club stepped up to lead a campaign to restore and maintain the garden and buildings. Its goal was for the property to benefit people of all ages through education, active involvement, and enjoyment of "the tranquil setting of an urban garden."

There were numerous challenges to succeed in the political arena, as interest groups lobbied for a variety of uses for the Gamble property. These included everything from an additional lawn bowling green, artists' studio space or teen center in the house, to selling the property for development of subsidized senior or low-income housing.

Thoughtful and protracted discussions on these wide-ranging ideas were held over a four-year period. With the city's permission, the Garden Club organized their members and other volunteers in clearing and re-planting what had become a shambles of a garden. Others made enough improvements in the house for a designer showcase that benefited the American Cancer Society. So far the wrecking ball, a solution advanced by a few, had been dodged.

As measures were taken to shore up the Gamble property, members of the Garden Club recognized the enormity of what they were taking on and began to formalize additional support. To carry out their campaign a Founding Board of Directors was created, made up of leaders from their organization and like-minded community members. A comprehensive proposal was crafted and neighborhood and community-wide support were enlisted. A fund-raising effort was launched to help secure the future of what they hoped would become the Elizabeth F. Gamble Garden, a non-profit foundation.

ABOVE LEFT *Miss Gamble as a young woman.* ABOVE RIGHT *Miss Gamble's favorite flower was the Iris. In 1994, hybridizer Lois O'Brien, a long-time friend, created the Iris 'Elizabeth Gamble' shown here growing next to the Gamble House.*

OPPOSITE *An aerial view of the Gamble property today. It is within walking distance of downtown Palo Alto and Stanford University. Gamble Garden occupies the acreage to the left, approximately two-thirds of the block. The open green area on the right is the Palo Alto Lawn Bowls Club with adjacent Palo Alto City Park areas.*

Before making its decision, the Palo Alto City Council, having already received years of input, entertained extensive public discussion. At City Hall in May 1985, "Of the hundreds of people who packed the chambers and overflowed into the foyer, almost seventy requested time to address the council," reported the *Peninsula Times Tribune*. The huge response necessitated a delay in the council's final action.

A week later, on May thirteenth, with another overflow crowd, Gamble Garden supporters wore flowers to the fateful City Council meeting. They came to witness the outcome that would determine the future of the Gamble property. When the vote was taken at midnight the nearly unanimous result was to create the proposed community horticultural center.

This talented, persuasive group of people had worked artfully and tirelessly toward their goal, sustained by their vision and optimism. One of their leaders later remarked, "We were a group of people who didn't know we couldn't do it." That same determined spirit was needed for the task ahead—to rescue the neglected property. Initially the city granted the fledgling group a trial period which later became multiple-year leases.

Who were the people behind this garden and house that generated such intense interest almost eighty years after it was built and had fallen into serious disrepair? Elizabeth's father, Edwin Percy Gamble (1852-1939) was the youngest son of James Gamble, co-founder of Procter & Gamble. Edwin and his wife Elizabeth, called Lilla, (1847-1927) moved from Kentucky to Palo Alto in 1902, a year after the family visited the area where their oldest son, James, attended Stanford University. James and his brothers George and Launcelot all graduated from Stanford. Elizabeth Frances, born in 1888 and the only daughter, was the next-to-youngest of the four children and thirteen years old when the Gambles settled in California.

ABOVE *The horse-drawn carriage for a wedding party brings back a bygone era. The property is a popular venue for events and celebrations.*

OPPOSITE *Viewed through a local store-front window, the display features a Gamble Art in the Garden event. Passersby are attracted by the garden-themed display with the backdrop mural of Gamble and a painting of Gamble on the easel.*

After graduating from Harker Day School, Elizabeth spent a year abroad, most of it living with extended family in Ireland, the original home of her great-grandfather Gamble. During her stay, she also toured Europe with an aunt, including a visit with the King of Prussia with whom she practiced her German.

Back in California, Elizabeth attended Stanford for a year, and then continued her studies in German at Wellesley College in Massachusetts. After graduating, she returned to the family home in Palo Alto in 1910. Settling there permanently after college, the young Elizabeth became involved in the community and began a life-long interest in the garden. Early on she worked with the three gardeners her parents employed. Over the years, Elizabeth put her own imprint on the garden. She introduced new horticultural species including trees shipped from the New York Botanical Garden and her native Kentucky.

The year that Elizabeth returned to live in the family home, Palo Alto's new three-story hospital had been completed on the lot behind the Gambles' house. As the community grew, a larger hospital, the Hoover Pavilion, was built in 1931 on Stanford University land. The abandoned property adjacent to the Gambles prompted interest in various uses—a prescient civic exercise for this plot of land. A movement to form the Palo Alto Lawn Bowls Club finally won approval. With help in planning from John McLaren, Superintendent of San Francisco's Golden Gate Park, the construction of the Club was done by Depression-era Civil Works Administration laborers in 1934. The Club became the Gambles' new over-the-garden-fence neighbor. Today, Gamble Garden and the lawn bowlers continue to occupy the same city block. They remain complementary occupants, jointly offering a gentler pace of life.

ABOVE *The Gamble House in the early nineteen-hundreds.*
OPPOSITE *The Palo Alto Lawn Bowls Club is Gamble Garden's back-fence neighbor.*

Philanthropy took many forms in the Gamble family. Elizabeth's civic contributions, like those of her family, made her a much-appreciated volunteer and benefactor. Along with giving her time and talent, she financed college educations for several local students. In 1925, two years before Elizabeth's mother died, her parents donated the money to build a parish hall for All Saints' Episcopal Church. Elizabeth was a long-time superintendent of the Sunday School at All Saints' and taught in the program for forty years.

As a founding member of the Stanford-Palo Alto Hospital Auxiliary, where she served for thirty-five years in various positions, Elizabeth donated baskets of her flowers for patients' rooms. Over the years, she continued to share the garden's bounty by leaving containers of cut flowers next to her fence for neighbors to help themselves. It was Elizabeth who had, after her parents' deaths, planted a large cutting garden, plowing up the orchard and the pony ring where she had ridden as a child.

Today the cutting garden is a favorite place for visitors. It remains a source of abundant flowers used in weekly fresh arrangements in the house and for special events. Continuing the tradition of sharing, flowers from the garden are used in floral bouquets made by members of the Garden Club of Palo Alto and distributed throughout the community to hospitals, schools, and public service offices.

In 1948 Miss Gamble, as she came to be known, added a Tea House with patio and surrounding garden, all designed by landscape designer Allan Himes Reid, and intended as a location for meetings. The cozy structure with a brick fireplace and wall of sliding glass doors was in keeping with mid-century architecture, western indoor-outdoor living, and a departure from the style of the 1902 house. In the spirit of Miss Gamble's activities, this area is still much used for Gamble events, with the Tea House serving as a flower arranging area and a meeting place for the Roots & Shoots intergenerational garden program.

Elizabeth Gamble continued to share her home and garden, forging meaningful friendships throughout her life. While she avoided the limelight, some of Miss Gamble's actions became known. Her relationship with the Noro family in Palo Alto offers personal insight into her character and the times, and a link to the earlier and later years of Gamble Garden. During World War II, Mrs. Noro, a widow who was Miss Gamble's housekeeper, was sent to Japanese internment camps. Miss Gamble visited Mrs. Noro at the Santa Anita camp. Meanwhile Mrs. Noro's son, Seiki Noro, a California native, served in the

TOP LEFT *Fresh-cut flowers from the garden are arranged for public service locations by the Garden Club of Palo Alto.*
BOTTOM RIGHT *The grotto, designed by Albert Wilson for the Allée, was commissioned by Miss Gamble and built around 1937. It was restored in the 1980s.*

U.S. Army. During the war, Miss Gamble oversaw the rental of the Noro house and deposited the money in an account for her housekeeper.

Following the war Mrs. Noro returned to the Gamble home and Seiki resumed his studies at the University of Washington. When Mrs. Noro later became ill and could no longer work, her son returned to Palo Alto to be with her. Along with paying Mrs. Noro's medical bills, Miss Gamble hired Seiki as an assistant to her gardeners. Seiki continued working at the Gamble property until Miss Gamble's death and stayed on afterwards, eventually becoming a staff member at the newly formed horticultural foundation. During his lengthy tenure, Seiki was both a witness to and a participant in the garden's evolution. In 1999, by then in his early eighties, Seiki was celebrated for his fifty years in the garden. His many friends honored his legacy with an endowment brick in the Gazebo.

ABOVE *The Tea House, with patio and fountain along the brick wall, was added by Miss Gamble in 1948 for meetings and entertaining. The small building and patio are versatile spaces that continue to be well used.*

What began as a family home became a hub of community and horticultural activity. Those antecedents were the inspiration for what Gamble Garden is today—a nurturing place for plants and people. In its new incarnation, Gamble Garden is open to the public every day for enjoyment and learning. It is sustained and maintained by a small paid staff and a long roster of volunteers who work tens of thousands of hours every year. For its financial support Gamble Garden relies, as it has from the beginning, completely on private funding.

ABOVE *The bronze endowment medallion was laid in 1997 and is the centerpiece of the Gazebo's brick floor. Bricks are engraved with the names of those who make major contributions to the Endowment Fund or the names of those they wish to honor with their donations.*

Gamble is formally classified as a rehabilitated garden, rather than a restored garden. This designation accounts for the extensive alterations made by Miss Gamble over many decades and significant changes made later to accommodate the needs of a modern public garden.

GAMBLE CHANGES OVER THE YEARS

Restored or retained from the early 1900s:

> Formal garden rooms connected by paths
> Semi-circular driveway
> Foundation plantings
> Hedges
> Fencing in natural wood
> Water features

**Alterations from the early 1900s
through the mid-1900s:**

> Carriage House converted to garage
> Orchard, kitchen garden, and pony
> ring converted to flower cutting beds
> Tea House built

Major changes since the 1980s:

> Entire garden completely re-done
> Garage converted to event space with separate kitchen
> Horticultural office, storage area, and public restrooms built
> Lath House and Greenhouse rebuilt
> Fencing replaced, modeled after the original
> Living fence of espaliered fruit trees added
> Roots & Shoots intergenerational gardens added
> Gazebo built
> Heritage plants re-introduced

ABOVE *Fred wandered into the garden and liked
what he saw. He was lovingly received and stayed on
to look after Gamble for more than ten years.*

AT GAMBLE GARDEN

Gamble Garden is open every day of the year during daylight hours at no charge and offers:

DOCENT TOURS of the house
& garden on weekdays & use of
the HORTICULTURAL REFERENCE LIBRARY

GARDEN-RELATED CLASSES
open to the public for modest fees

RENTALS of Gamble House public
rooms, Carriage House & Patios
for meetings & social events

WEDDING COORDINATING SERVICES

ANNUAL SPRING TOUR of local private
gardens, with Gamble boutique & luncheon

ANNUAL EARTH DAY CELEBRATION

LUNCHEONS & RECEPTIONS

HOLIDAY GREENS SALES of fresh-cut greens,
planted bulbs, & fresh arrangements made
by Gamble's master floral designers

TOP RIGHT *A volunteer working in the Rose Garden.*
BOTTOM LEFT *A pink Spider Chrysanthemum.*

PLANT SALES several times a year of plants grown at Gamble

ROOTS & SHOOTS on-site intergenerational garden program led by Gamble volunteers for third-graders from a neighborhood school

CHILDREN'S ACTIVITIES include story-time in the garden, puppet shows, Easter egg hunt, Halloween haunted house, & birthday parties

COMMUNITY DAY autumn garden activities & resources for all ages

MASTER GARDENERS available weekly for consultation in person & by phone

GAMBLE WEB SITE information about events & classes

BLOOM ALERTS announce what is currently flowering

MEMBERSHIP benefits include newsletter, discounts on class fees & some ticketed events, discounts at nurseries, florists, & garden supply businesses

VOLUNTEER OPPORTUNITIES to work in the gardens, at fund-raising events, & in an array of responsibilities that keep Gamble Garden humming along

ABOVE *The frog fountain delights all ages.*

NEW PATHWAYS
in an OLD GARDEN

A WALK THROUGH THE GARDEN

A garden is a sanctuary as well as a creation . . . a spiritual and a physical refuge more transforming than I'd ever imagined it to be.

—MIRABEL OSLER

Gamble Garden unfolds in an inviting arrangement of garden rooms and distinctively planted areas. Beginning in the mid-nineteen-eighties, the stewards of the original garden have succeeded in preserving and recreating its strengths and enhancing it with creative alterations. Like the narrative of any evolving garden, there are the joys and trials of choosing the best plants for the right locations, nurturing all that thrive, and responding to the unexpected.

OPPOSITE *A view of Gamble Garden toward the white Gazebo from inside the house. The porch leads to the library. The Wisteria Garden begins to the right.*

A   Entry and Front Lawn

B   Formal Garden Border

C   Allée

D   House Plantings

E   Rose Garden Entry

F   Rose Garden

G   Carriage House and Patio

H   Wisteria Garden

I   Tea House and Patio

J   Woodland Area

K   Propagation Area

L   Roots & Shoots

M   Shade and Sun Garden

N   Shade Garden

O   Mediterranean Garden

P   Perennial Borders

Q   Demonstration Beds

R   Iris Bed

S   Cutting Garden

T   Formal Herb Garden

U   Grand Oak Area

V   Orchard Area

W   California-Style Garden Room

X   Parking Area Plantings

Y   Kellogg Parkette and
       Native Garden

Z   Waverley and Churchill
       Sidewalk Gardens

B   Bike Racks

P   Parking

R   Restrooms

Embarcadero Road

(EXIT)

Horticulturist Office

Gazebo

ENTRANCE

P

B

R

Greenhouse

Carriage House

G

K

F

E

Churchill Avenue

I

H

D

B

House

J

C

Z

A

Gamble House

A

Waverley Street

Z

THE GARDEN ROOMS

Three areas of Gamble are garden rooms—the Allée, the Wisteria Garden, and the Rose Garden. Creating garden rooms on a two-and-a-third acre property was not typical in the early twentieth century, and that early imprint on the land around the Gamble family's three-story house is as noteworthy today as it was then.

The enclosed garden rooms provide a unique experience for enjoying the character and plants in each space. Crossing the threshold into each garden room brings you to a new scene with treasures at every turn. The walls of the garden room can be made of wood, stone, shrubs, trees, or any combination of these.

The Allée

The Allée features Weeping Japanese Flowering Cherry trees (*Prunus x subhirtella* 'Pendula'), an arresting sight in any season and a contemplative world unto itself. At one end of the divided rows of trees is a Canary Island Date Palm (*Phoenix canariensis*). The palm shades a teak bench, a favorite stopping place. From the vantage point of the bench is a view of the Gamble family sundial, original to the garden, partway down the path. Anchoring the path's end is a stone grotto fountain with water-friendly plants, a magnet for birds and children.

Profuse blooms in springtime on the cherry trees create a nimbus of pink that gradually gives way to the shade of dense, green umbrella-like branches in summer. In winter the grafts at the tops of the trunks are easiest to spot, and the arching bare branches create a line of descent toward the ground in graceful water-fountain fashion.

The surrounding Boxwood (*Buxus sempervirens*) hedges are light green in spring and deepen in the summer to a gray-blue green. Year round, they provide a tidy border for a carpet of *Vinca minor* interspersed with spring bulbs.

TOP *The Allée and the first daffodils in late winter.*
BOTTOM *In full spring bloom, the bench invites lingering.*
OPPOSITE *In summer, the Allée is a palette of greens.*

The Wisteria Garden

In case you are still puzzled by the difference between the Chinese and Japanese wisterias, compare the way the stems twist. The Japanese go clockwise, the Chinese anti-clockwise. I wish I knew what message this is intended to convey.

—Thomas Pakenham

The Wisteria Garden, a popular location for intimate weddings, is behind the Gamble House where the library and back porch offer an ideal view of this favorite area. Enclosed by wood fencing on the remaining three sides, it features Double Lavender Japanese Wisteria plants (*W. floribunda* 'Violacea-Plena'), some original and others propagated from cuttings.

Inside the rows of wisteria is an encircling brick path lined with boxwood hedges framing shade-loving perennials, annuals, and bulbs. A single wisteria (*W. floribunda* 'Purpurea') thrives near the fountain. The delicate sounds of splashing water draw attention to this focal point.

A Paperbark Maple (*Acer griseum*) is found in the Wisteria Garden. Distinguished by reddish, peeling, paper-like bark, the effect brings chocolate curls to mind. Peeling is a way for these trees to shed toxins, a characteristic shared by some birch trees.

Other trees and shrubs in this garden room include Weeping Cherry (*Prunus x subhirtella* 'Pendula'), Banana Shrub (*Michelia figo*), Varigated Privet (*Ligustrum*), Deutzia (*D. scabra* 'Pride of Rochester'), and a pair of Magnolias (*M. 'Star Wars'*).

TOP *Wisteria and boxwood hedge line the brick path.* BOTTOM *The trunk of the Paperbark Maple is an arresting sight with its thin peels of brown bark.* OPPOSITE *Tulips add to the late spring show in the Wisteria Garden with a view toward the back of the house.*

The Rose Garden

Won't you come into my garden? I'd like my roses to see you.

—Richard Sheridan

The Rose Garden room is set off by Gamble's signature tall lattice fencing on all four sides. The geometry of the space—a circle within a rectangle—is defined by heritage roses, which were reintroduced to the garden, and modern roses along the border fence. A wide circular path and a ring of all white roses (*R. 'Iceberg'*) surround the interior lawn. The room is furnished with teak garden benches for its frequent visitors and is another popular setting for wedding ceremonies.

The center of the Rose Garden was designed originally for the game known as Clock Golf. This quick round of golf was popular in England beginning in the mid-1800s. To play, twelve markers, each representing an hour on the clock face, are placed around the perimeter of a circular lawn approximately twenty to twenty-four feet in diameter. Starting at the one o'clock position, players putt from each hour marker into a container set within the circle, but not in the center.

TOP *A lush wall of mixed roses looking toward the Allée.* RIGHT *A multi-layered Rose Garden lattice wall with Rosa 'Sparrieshoop.'* OPPOSITE *The entrance to the circular Rose Garden is defined by an arbor. R. 'Iceberg' roses encircle the lawn, framed by Catmint (Nepeta x faassenii).*

Entry & Front Lawn

It is worth any amount of effort to be able to see your house through the arch of a tree.

—Thomas D. Church

No longer used for horse and carriage, the entry to the house and front lawn is defined by a semi-circular drive with the original iron gates still in place. The adjoining hedges and nearby painted fences are characteristic of the house's era. Two grand Southern Magnolias (*M. grandiflora*)—horticultural foreigners in this Mediterranean climate—grace the front lawn. They are notable for their leathery foliage, large blossoms, and interesting surface root structure. In the early nineteen hundreds a local women's group planted Southern Magnolias on a number of streets in Palo Alto where they continue to thrive.

Two Canary Island Date Palms (*Phoenix canariensis*)—of the three originally planted on the property—recall the interest in exotic plants at the time the garden was established. In place for more than one hundred years, these noble sentries are arboreal exclamation points in the garden.

To the right of the house, a shrub border frames the adjacent Allée. The border includes viburnum, pittosporum, and loropetalum of varying heights, textures, and colors. Seasonal interest comes from the yellow summer catkins and autumn color of the Chinese Tallow tree (*Sapium sebiferum*).

In late summer, when the cutting garden flowers are nearly exhausted from providing months of continuous color, our heads are turned toward a new show. The Crape Myrtles (*Lagerstroemia*) are scene-stealers. They draw our eyes upward, where vivid magenta blooms begin at the tree tops, high above the garden floor, against a brilliant azure sky. The exfoliating bark provides additional interest. Nearby, autumn summons the fragrance of the small flowers of the Sweet Olive shrub (*Osmanthus fragrans*) and the rich colors of the Japanese Maples (*Acer palmatum*).

Woodland Area

The woodland area offers an arresting view from inside the Gamble House and from several approaches throughout the garden. In this location are varieties of camellia, rhododendron, azalea, and hydrangea plants, along with the dogwood tree. In winter, a sculptural arc is formed from the Persimmon tree (*Diospyros kaki* 'Hachiya'), and on through the series of deciduous *Magnolia x soulangeana*. The nearby shade garden is a lushly planted area showcasing the textures of ferns, hellebores, Japanese anemone, and hydrangea. Also found here is the unusual cucumber tree (*Magnolia acuminata subcordata*).

ABOVE *The front lawn entrance to the woodland area offers a showy display of Magnolia x soulangeana trees in early spring.* OPPOSITE *A Canary Island Date Palm crown seen through an early spring wreath of Southern Magnolia, left, and Japanese Maple, right.*

Heritage Plants

Some of the most cherished plants at Gamble are ones from the early 1900s that were original to the garden. These heritage plants continue to grow today and others are being reintroduced to the garden after a long absence. Receipts from Miss Gamble's purchases, books, and drawings have been researched to discover plants to return to the garden. These new additions come from sources all over the United States and include varieties of camellias, rhododendrons, viburnums, and tree peonies.

Camellia sasanqua 'Fukuzutsumi' (Apple Blossom) was purchased by Miss Gamble in 1943. Eight of these have been reintroduced at the front side of the house, where they form a hedge with single soft white flowers flushed with pink. The Gambles also favored plants such as the *Osmanthus fragrans aurantiacus* and *Rhaphiolepis umbellata* around the house foundation, and more of both have been added in the heritage planting project.

Along with their winter and spring floral colors and important role in the garden throughout the year, the stories of camellias add to their interest. For example, *Camellia japonica* 'Haikaru Genji' (Brilliant Genji) 1859, purchased by Miss Gamble in 1938 and located outside the library, is named for the romantic hero of the early Japanese novel *The Tale of Genji* by Lady Murasaki Shikibu. Also in the garden is the 1695 *Camellia japonica* 'Hagoromo' (Feathered Robe), with blush pink flowers. In Japanese folklore, a feathered robe is the traditional raiment of an angel. This fragrant informal double camellia is dark salmon-pink, bordered in white, and streaked with scarlet. Gamble Garden, with its large and varied camellia collection, is part of the American Camellia Society Trail.

ABOVE *The Chinese tree peony (Paeonia suffruticosa 'Reine Elizabeth')*
was purchased by Miss Gamble in 1938 and has been reintroduced
into the garden. The blue-green markers make it easy to locate heritage
plants throughout the garden.

Succulents

The succulent collection occupies a small part of the garden, but its location and the popularity of the plants draw a lot of attention. Artistically planted containers are sought after at Gamble's plant sales.

The main succulent bed is adjacent to a long fence where espaliered apple trees grow on the reverse side. The fruit trees provide shade for the succulent varieties that are less tolerant of afternoon sun. For added interest, the succulents' architectural shapes and range of colors are mixed with other types of companion plants.

TOP *The Lath House is a propagation area and nursery for succulents.* CENTER *Grassy wisps contrast with Graptoveria 'Fred Ives' in the succulent bed.* BOTTOM *An outline of cream and blush pink distinguish Aeonium 'Sunburst'.*

Carriage House & Patio

The Carriage House was originally for the family horses and carriages. Remodeled in 1987, it is now used for Gamble classes and events, and rented for business seminars and private social gatherings.

The prominent tree in front of the Carriage House is a Scarlet Oak (*Quercus coccinea*), planted in 1989. Native to the northeastern United States, this deciduous tree provides spectacular fall color. Its leaves turn brown and die in winter but remain on the tree until spring when new leaves emerge. Nearby are several varieties of Japanese maple, each with a different leaf color and leaf shape.

In a nearby corner is the Turk's Cap (*Malvaviscus arboreus var. mexicana*), a red flowering shrub in the Mallow family, popular at the turn of the twentieth century.

TOP *The Scarlet Oak in mid-summer provides extensive shade. The Carriage House glows at dusk from its interior lighting.* RIGHT *Autumn color of the Scarlet Oak on the Carriage House Patio.*

Tea House & Patio

In 1948, Miss Gamble commissioned landscape architect Allan Himes Reid to design the Tea House and Patio as a meeting place for community groups and it is still widely used today. Notable here are the Chinese Fringe Tree (*Chionanthus retusus*), the Climbing Hydrangea (*H. anomala petiolaris*), and the trellis-trained Cat's Claw Vine (*Macfadyena unguis-cati*).

At the back of the Tea House is a Cockspur Coral Tree (*Erythrina crista-galli*), Argentina's national tree. Planted by the Gamble family, it is pruned annually by pollarding. A rare tree in this area, it requires several mild winters and a sheltered location to become established and to bloom.

TOP *Coral tree blossoms.* RIGHT *The endearing seven-foot tall topiary rabbit is made of English boxwood. Against the brick wall are espaliered pear trees.*

Gazebo & Perennial Border

. . . June 21st
today is the beginning of summer
two or three birds
invent a garden.

—OCTAVIO PAZ

The Gazebo, added in 1996, has become an iconic symbol for Gamble Garden and a Palo Alto landmark. The attached seats inside each of the lattice corners face the Gazebo interior where readers, children, and anyone stopping to enjoy the garden are often found.

Under the Gazebo is the Endowment Fund bronze medallion and an expanding collection of donor bricks representing major financial gifts to Gamble. Every brick has a story and each one bears the names of the donors or those whom they wish to honor.

Horticulturally, the structure supports vertical gardening. Its vines include Sweet Autumn Clematis (*C. terniflora*) and Porcelain Berry (*Ampelopsis brevipedunculata*).

Extending out from the Gazebo in two directions, the perennial border is a varied collection of plants in a range of colors, forms, and textures, with no plants taller than five feet. The design for these beds takes into consideration how they are captured when photographed and painted. The beds are planted in color schemes, each in shades of a particular color, sometimes with the complimentary color included.

Examples of some of the old-fashioned flowers that might be found here are Joe Pye weed (*Eupatorium purpureum*), daylily (*Hemerocallis*), and bearded iris.

ABOVE *Friends share time and reading by the perennial garden.*
OPPOSITE *The Gamble Garden Gazebo in summer bloom.*

Grand Oak Area

The canopy of the Coast Live Oak (*Quercus agrifolia*)—estimated to be 200 years old—shades a large space in this area of the garden. Although truly an evergreen, its leaves persist for only one year, then fall from the tree when new growth starts in the spring. The setting, with no under-planting and no irrigation, is ideal for this tree and the amply sheltered picnic tables.

Beneath the expansive oak branches is a small formal herb garden originally created by the Herb Study Guild of Palo Alto. With its boxwood border and a central birdbath, the bench facing the perennial garden invites lingering in this island-like setting. The area nearby is planted with savory herbs and species geraniums against a backdrop of Butterfly Bush (*Buddleia*) and Smoke Tree (*Cotinus coggygria*). The dense planting also has varieties of Sage (*Salvia*), a collection of Hyssop (*Agastache*), and a Chaste Tree (*Vitex agnus-castus*).

*I don't know when tree houses for adults went out of fashion
— and still less why. I myself would rather have an arboreal
retreat than a swimming pool any day.*

—ELEANOR PERENYI

The diminutive structure in a back corner is like a tree house come to earth. It is made entirely of bare twigs, from its layered cone-shaped roof and throughout its woven dark enclosure. Walking through the grand oak area, one is drawn to the willow hut, a place that intrigues young and old.

Inside its secretive shelter, with room for only two or three people, it is a magical place. Gamble has learned that, from time to time, fairies issue invitations to a child and an adult companion to attend a fairy tea in the willow hut. The fairies are too shy to make an appearance, but from their hiding places they take great pleasure in their guests' delight.

ABOVE *The willow hut in the lushly planted grand oak area.*
OPPOSITE *The herb garden and the grand oak tree.*

In 2000 Gamble Garden became steward of this one-third acre parcel. Facing a major thoroughfare, the parkette provides a grassy setback that buffers the Gamble House and garden from traffic and introduces the garden to passersby with a California native garden. The area, renovated in 2005 with resources from local Rotary Clubs, offers meandering paths among both sunny and shaded planting beds.

A recent addition to the garden is the Fernleaf Catalina Ironwood tree (*Lyonothamnus floribundus asplenifolius*), native to the Channel Islands off the Southern California coast. A nearby neighbor is a California Buckeye (*Aesculus californica*), a deciduous tree with striking cream-colored, fragrant flower plumes in spring that are toxic to bees. In the fall this variety grows the largest fruit of all the Buckeyes in the world. The big pear-shaped fruit splits naturally to reveal shiny brown seeds and are favorites for floral arrangements.

TOP *A vivid spring flowering of daffodils, Ceanothus 'Dark Star', and flowering crabapple in the parkette.*
RIGHT *Volunteers install the new landscaping.*
OPPOSITE *Viewed from a busy intersection, the parkette beckons toward the quiet garden beyond the fence.*

Fruit Trees

Gamble encourages native bees—ones not inclined to sting—in the orchard and elsewhere, including the Roots & Shoots area, to promote a pollinator garden. This is achieved by leaving uncovered spaces on the ground for the bees to create holes and become established in the garden. They are also welcomed by small wooden bee condominiums on posts a few feet above ground.

Antique varieties of apples and pears are espaliered along fences and against some of the outbuilding walls. Espaliering is sculpturally appealing and an efficient use of space in a small garden. The compact form increases fruit production and provides year-round interest with blossoms, fruit, seasonal foliage, and dramatic bare branches in winter.

Next to the Horticulturist Office, along with citrus trees, is the Fig tree (*Ficus carica* 'Black Mission'), a popular fruit and common tree in the Bay Area. The Black Mission variety produces purple-black fruit with pink flesh that is delicious either fresh or dried. The tree is fertilized by the fig wasp that goes inside the fruit where the female wasp dies, and the male escapes.

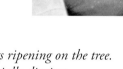

Nearby is an Asian Pear tree (*Pyrus pyrifolia* 'Hosui'). Although not an apple hybrid, the round fruit, unlike European pears, is apple-shaped and has a crispy texture. In the front garden, the Japanese Persimmon (*Diospyros kaki* 'Hachiya') fruit ripens in late fall and early winter, well after the tree's leaves have turned gold and fallen.

TOP LEFT *Asian pears.* BOTTOM LEFT *Japanese persimmon tree.* BOTTOM RIGHT *Figs ripening on the tree.*
OPPOSITE *The youngest visitors to Gamble have a natural affinity for gardening, especially digging.*

TENDING
and GROUNDSKEEPING

GAMBLE GARDENERS AT WORK

I have drifted farther and farther from my muse, closer and closer to my post-hole digger.

—E. B. WHITE

Garden is both noun and verb, a place and an activity. Gamble Garden is a horticultural gem thanks to a dedicated, knowledgeable team of volunteer gardeners and staff horticulturists. Long before a fine-tuned maintenance program was in place, the first ambitious volunteers in the early nineteen-eighties invested countless hours of hands-on labor and rescued the garden from its neglected state. Landscape professionals have been essential to the garden's successful rehabilitation and in shaping its new design elements.

OPPOSITE *A garden volunteer.*

A small part-time staff provides planning for the garden and leads the volunteers who work thousands of hours each year. Whenever a garden area requires renovation, and when innovations are undertaken, the gardeners' goals are to keep the heritage garden area as close to its original plan as possible and for overall design integrity throughout.

TOP LEFT *A robust brown Cymbidium orchid growing in the Lath House.*
TOP RIGHT *Garden volunteers consult and plan.*
BOTTOM LEFT *A wall planter of mixed succulents hangs at the Lath House entrance.*
OPPOSITE *The highs and lows of garden volunteers.*

Guided by thoughtful plans and best garden practices in the day-to-day maintenance and monthly tasks, garden volunteers water wisely—essential in a Mediterranean climate—and mount pest defensives using non-toxic methods. They dig, amend the soil, plant, transplant, and pull up weeds. They trim and prune artfully and precisely. They rake, sweep, and compost. They propagate from on-site cuttings, tuck some into cold frames for special protection, and nurture new plants in the Greenhouse and Lath House. They pot and re-pot and move pots as needed for the best location. They maintain paths, patios, fences, and fountains. They work hard in all kinds of weather and have a good time. They reap great personal rewards from their work, and everyone is rewarded with a beautiful garden to enjoy.

While the garden is beautifully maintained, some materials, such as fallen seed pods and low branches, are left in place to encourage wildlife habitat formation. The presence of birds, animals, and insects enriches the garden and the garden experience.

ABOVE LEFT *Seedlings are transplanted into cell packs, a step in preparation for eventual planting in the garden.* ABOVE RIGHT *Lettuce ready for the garden after starting in the Greenhouse, or Lath House, or in a cold frame.*

OPPOSITE: TOP *The tool shed is well equipped and carefully maintained for year-round garden work.* BOTTOM LEFT *An orchid grows in the protective environment of the Greenhouse.* BOTTOM RIGHT *Garden stakes for plant identification are important sources of information for both gardeners and visitors at Gamble.*

A specialty at Gamble are espaliered fruit trees, an aesthetic method for making the most of limited spaces. Annual precision pruning maintains the unique shape over the years, increases fruit production, and offers arresting displays of the trees' changes over four seasons. Heritage apple trees, planted in 1989, grow against a backdrop of the green fencing that outlines the garden. Nearby, pear trees grow on metal supports against the horticultural office and on the back brick wall of the Tea House. The extra fruit harvest is donated to local food banks.

TOP LEFT *Seven varieties of apple trees with spring blossoms.* TOP RIGHT *A Pyrus communis 'Seckel' European Pear in early spring.* BOTTOM LEFT *Pyrus communis 'Duchess d'Angouleme' European Pear trees in the fall.* BOTTOM RIGHT *Espaliered apple trees in winter.* OPPOSITE *The Lath House interior just after its completion.*

SPRING TOUR

INSPIRATION FROM PRIVATE GARDENS AROUND US

I know a bank whereon the wild thyme blows,
Where oxlips and the nodding violet grows,
Quite over-canopied with luscious woodbine,
With sweet musk roses and with eglantine...

—WILLIAM SHAKESPEARE

Gardens, forever inspiring and never finished, have a hold on us. We forge ahead in garden art and science, whether tending a pot of herbs on a balcony or managing an intricately designed grand spread. Often the call of spring leads us away from our piece of earth to visit other gardens, learn, marvel, and set our gardening sights ever higher. These excursions renew us for keeping our own Edens thriving.

OPPOSITE, SCENES FROM SPRING TOUR:
FAR LEFT, TOP *A faux bois bench beckons from a secluded destination.*
FAR LEFT, BOTTOM *The carved pedestal is a focal point and offers contrasting texture in a knot garden.*
NEAR LEFT, TOP *Oversized tools in a large, colorful pot add unexpected wit to a traditional garden.*
NEAR LEFT, CENTER *At Gamble, a bouquet welcomes visitors into the house.*
NEAR LEFT, BOTTOM *Many suburban gardeners are enjoying and benefiting from keeping chickens. Roomy and well-appointed coops are given pride of place in landscape designs.*

Each year, Spring Tour is a highlight on the Gamble Garden calendar and in the community. The two-day public fundraising event for the garden began in 1986 and is attended by garden enthusiasts from near and far. It is an ideal time to visit and learn from local private gardens, see the Gamble property in its spring finery, and enjoy garden-related activities.

Following months of preparations, generous residents welcome the public to visit their gardens. On tour days visitors engage in the pleasures of garden conversation with docents who populate each garden. An informative guidebook includes the history of each garden. Landscape narratives cover details about each garden's design and plants of special interest.

SPRING TOUR GARDENS

ABOVE LEFT *A succulent-filled urn by a lily pond with papyrus plants in the background.*
ABOVE RIGHT *A bold color for the gate creates an uplifting accent in the garden.*
OPPOSITE *A well-used greenhouse takes pride of place in a Palo Alto garden.*

Details from Private
Gardens
on Spring Tour

TOP LEFT *Blue glass and 22k gold inset tiles accent a swimming pool*
oasis in a back garden. TOP RIGHT *A mighty acorn sculpture—the*
unexpected and fanciful. BOTTOM LEFT *Propping open the gate is accomplished*
with wit and charm. OPPOSITE *A close-up look at an extensive piquet*
assiette mural that enlivens the basement stairwell walls leading from the garden.

Views of Private
Gardens on

TOP LEFT *The rooster weather vane is used decoratively in a rustic setting.*
TOP RIGHT *An iron gate takes the functional to the artistic.*
BOTTOM LEFT *A Buddha head—made by the owners' son, a professional sculptor—poised on a tall tree stump.*

the Gamble Garden
Spring Tour

TOP LEFT *A playhouse in the shade with a handy bucket and a blue slide for quick exiting.*
TOP RIGHT *The vertical ivy and pineapple sage fit into small spaces and complement the Tudor-style door.*
BOTTOM RIGHT *Useful and pleasing combinations are made by pairing vegetables and accent flowers.*

~ 67 ~

TOP LEFT *The rose climber in full bloom clings to a salvaged iron spiral staircase support, spilling over the top—a stairway to the sky, or as the homeowners call it, 'Waiting for Godot.'*

TOP RIGHT *An open ironwork window box showcases ornamental kale and flowers. The rustic container is thickly lined with Spanish moss adding more texture and color and serving as a screen for the interior container.*

BOTTOM LEFT *Tables set for alfresco dining are often included in the private gardens. These settings complete the garden scenes and highlight another pleasure of outdoor living.*

BOTTOM RIGHT *The armillary, an ancient astronomical instrument, is a traditional favorite in gardens.*

LEFT *A view of the second story, above the entry, of an authentically-styled Tudor house built in the 1990s includes Cloud Nine Dogwood, Smoke Bush, and Lilac.*

RIGHT *Built in the 1920s, this Mediterranean style home on the Spring Tour has an inviting entry, where architectural elements are complemented by accent plants that include variegated holly, Graham Blandy boxwood, and Japanese boxwood. Beyond a front border of mature olive trees is trailing rosemary. Container plants include topiary and standards in ceramic, metal, and terra cotta pots.*

SPRING TOUR at GAMBLE

Master Gardeners and other guest experts are on hand to answer almost any garden question—everything from sustainable gardening to success with orchids. The popular plant sale at Gamble features plants grown on site, where knowledgeable volunteers are on hand to consult when making selections. A number of the plants chosen for the sale are based on those found in the tour gardens.

The Spring Tour Boutique features an array of wares inside the house and on the patio. Opening day attracts lines of shoppers eager to make purchases for their gardens and homes, purchases that also benefit Gamble.

In the Carriage House is a sale that began in the spirit of gardeners sharing seeds and cuttings. Known as Over the Garden Fence, the collection of donated garden items includes furniture, tools, containers—everything from the quirky to the sublime.

Advance orders are plentiful for gourmet box lunches, which can be enjoyed in the company of fellow garden lovers at tables set up around the garden. Members of the Garden Club of Palo Alto bake hundreds of cookies every year for Spring Tour. The outdoor refreshment table is a sought-out destination for enjoying their traditional tea thyme cookies.

The Spring Tour Silent Auction includes garden items, services, and entertaining ideas created by Gamble volunteers and friends. Most events take place at Gamble, or at the winning bidders' homes. Examples of featured offerings are:

- **Ladies' Luncheon and Bulb Potting** for 10 in a private English garden setting

- **Croquet Party for 20 at Gamble Garden** with spot-on refreshments

- **Garden Pruning** by Gamble experts will have your garden looking its best

- **Tip-Toe Through the Tulips** with 500 spring bulbs planted in your garden by Gamble's Garden Committee

- **Children's Garden Birthday Party** hosted at Gamble, with all the trimmings and garden games

- **Yoga Class and Brunch at Gamble** features restorative ohms and gourmet ahhs

- **Halloween Cocktail Party for 50** - come in costume to enjoy ghoulish drinks and gruesome appetizers at Gamble's annual Haunted House

- **A Year of Flowers** provides monthly cut flowers and greens for your home from Gamble, created by the Flower Arranging Committee

TOP *For sale, a bell jar mini garden created for Gamble by local designers.* RIGHT *Boutique items include note cards with images of Gamble made by local artists.* OPPOSITE: TOP RIGHT *Music on the lawn at Gamble.* BOTTOM LEFT *Spring Tour posters are placed around Palo Alto and neighboring communities. Each year a new design features the current theme.*

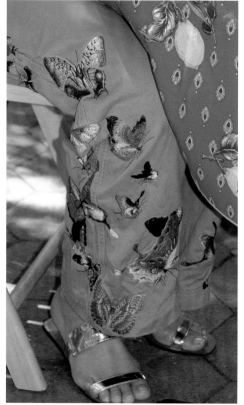

A Spring Tour Timeline

~

From Seed to Full Bloom

MAY ~ JUNE A year in advance, choose gardens for next year's tour. Sign up committee members. Establish budget.

JULY ~ AUGUST Photograph gardens selected for tour. Set meeting dates for the year.

SEPTEMBER ~ OCTOBER Spring Tour Committee begins monthly meetings. Send confirmation letters for tour to homeowners. Submit public relations listings. Secure commitments for silent auction and raffle.

TOP LEFT *A colorful front porch introduces visitors to a garden full of creative charm.* TOP RIGHT *With a putting green behind and a pool in front, inviting chairs are a place to sit and decide what to do next in a garden designed for family activity.* BOTTOM LEFT *A volunteer hostess dresses for the occasion. Hundreds of volunteers make this two-day event possible.*

NOVEMBER ~ DECEMBER Begin recruiting volunteers. Decide on caterer for tour lunch. Select boutique vendors.

JANUARY ~ FEBRUARY Mail letters for business and individual underwriting. Initiate public relations contacts with businesses. Write garden narratives with homeowners for guidebook. Choose graphics for guidebook. Meet with subcommittees. Write articles for the Gamble Newsletter.

MARCH Distribute tour posters. Mail tour brochures. Visit home gardens to coordinate plant sale held at Gamble.

EARLY APRIL Conduct orientation for additional volunteers. Send press kits and tour tickets to newspapers. Email flyer to volunteers and members for their distribution. Hang outside banner promoting tour. Mail tickets to pre-event purchasers.

MID-APRIL Volunteers tour the gardens where they will be hosts. Deliver notification letters to Gamble's neighbors. Label plants in private gardens.

SPRING TOUR WEEK
MONDAY ~ THURSDAY

Set up Over the Garden Fence in the Carriage House.

Complete table settings at tour gardens. Assist boutique vendors with set up. Prepare areas for silent auction and raffle. Set up plant sale.

Install signage at Gamble and each house on tour. Host Major Donors Preview Cocktail Party.

≈

FRIDAY & SATURDAY, TOUR DAYS

≈

TWO WEEKS AFTER TOUR

Host wrap-up party for Spring Tour Committee.

RIGHT *A Spring Tour private garden arbor with blooming white potato vine defines the threshold between garden areas.*

ART in the GARDEN

ARTISTS AT GAMBLE

Nothing is more the child of art than a garden.

—Sir Walter Scott

The artists' quest in the garden is to capture and interpret ephemeral blooms, steadfast trees, and seasonal changes. Some come with pencil and sketchpad or a full kit with easel, a rainbow of paint tubes, and an array of brushes. Others arrive with a tripod and bag of photography equipment, or a small camera tucked into a pocket. For all of them, the garden compels the artistic spirit.

OPPOSITE *An artist's setup at Gamble is a painterly attraction.*

TOP *A plein air painter finds his subjects in the ornamental beds.*
RIGHT *A well-used brush cleaning pot and easel set up for the artist's painting of hydrangeas.*

ABOVE LEFT *Visitors roam the gardens to talk with and watch artists at work and to attend the gallery display and sale of paintings held in the Gamble buildings.*
RIGHT: TOP AND BOTTOM *Artists' works in process.*

TOP *Gamble's profusion of tulips is always a big draw. At a Gamble floral photography class a student takes advantage of the spring spectacle.* RIGHT *A photographer aims toward the Gazebo, a popular subject.*

TOP *Like their adult counterparts, children with cameras find photo opportunities in the grand views and the details. Here, dwarf daffodils are eye-catching and picture-worthy.*

LEFT *Not all art in the garden is a work on canvas or paper. A Gamble art event with a strolling solo violinist.*

ROOTS & SHOOTS

INTERGENERATIONAL GARDEN

The best time I ever had in a garden . . .

—Roots & Shoots

Gardening at any age transcends soil and seed, relates in endless ways to life and learning, and brings pleasures both horticultural and personal. Having guided children and youth throughout her life, Miss Gamble would have loved Roots & Shoots—one of the earliest programs launched at Gamble Garden. The curriculum evolves, and volunteers of all ages participate, but always at the heart of it is leading children to become lifelong garden lovers, learning about plants, nature, and nutrition in an environment rich with sharing and fun.

OPPOSITE *Radishes from the Roots & Shoots garden, the freshest possible.*

DIGGING IN
The Start of the School Year

"The best time I ever had in a garden..." begins personal stories volunteers tell to introduce themselves to the third-grade students. Before long, the children will have their own "best time" stories to tell. The Roots, who are Gamble volunteers, teach the student Shoots the Gamble Garden song, a tune the students might be heard singing on their walks to and from the garden.

The Shoots learn to use garden tools—the right one for the right job and safety considerations—and how and why to clean

tools. To fully experience the gifts from a garden, the children are led on an Awareness Walk where they engage all five senses and talk about their experiences. By the end of their tour, they know the Gamble property, buildings, and the twenty-one Roots & Shoots garden beds where they will plant, tend, and harvest their crops. Working in small groups, students will become adept in all phases of gardening throughout the growing seasons.

TOP *A gardening team.*
RIGHT *Sign by the Roots & Shoots planting areas.*

A Year of Abundance

Gardening days can be planting and composting, propagating seeds, or forcing bulbs. The lessons are rounded out with sure-to-please activities that include songs, games, cooking, stories, poetry, craft projects, and role playing about garden topics.

Early in the school year, fall planting includes chard, kale, bok choy, Asian cabbage, mustard, potatoes, onions, lettuce, peas, snapdragons, and sweet peas. Spring planting choices include varieties of tomatoes, peppers, tomatilloes, cucumbers, squash, beans, lettuce, herbs; and from seed—carrots, beets, radishes, sunflowers, and cosmos. Each of the twenty-one beds is fifteen feet by three feet, and they are planted seasonally.

Shoots and their volunteer Roots experience the challenges and joys of the garden, harvest and prepare fresh foods that please their palates and expand their enjoyment of healthy eating. By intensively planting the garden, there is enough extra produce to donate to food banks—another way to share the garden's bounty.

ABOVE *Student and snail meet up in the greens.*

TOP LEFT *Showing off a just-picked green tomato.*
TOP RIGHT *A student prepares strawberries and peas.*
BOTTOM *Shoots give the taste test to salad made from their freshly harvested produce.*

Roots & Shoots Activities

ENJOYING FOODS FROM THE GARDEN Make popcorn in the fall ~ Toss salads in the spring ~ Grow culinary herbs for herbal tea and baking.

EARTHWORMS Earthworms—nature's plows—are observed with hand-held magnifying lenses. Findings are recorded and shared.

FLOWER PARTS AND POLLINATION Find out how flowers are seed factories, learn the role of bees, birds, wind, and butterflies; identify fragrance, color, and nectar. Labeling flower parts and solving a word puzzle are follow-up classroom activities.

CREATE A SUCCULENT DISH GARDEN Students learn about cacti and succulents and plant dish gardens, enhanced with decorative pebbles, to take home.

ACTION GAMES Meet a Tree ~ Noah's Ark ~ Owls and Crows ~ Amoeba Races

PICK HITS FROM THE ROOTS & SHOOTS SONG BOOK Dirt Made My Lunch ~ One-Ton Tomato ~ Savez-Vous Planter Des Choux? ~ I'm Too Full of Broccoli

GARDEN CRAFTS Sun Prints & Vegetable Stamp Printing ~ Pressed Flower Art Project ~ Cornhusk Dolls ~ Culinary Herbs, pressed and arranged under clear contact paper for making cookbook covers and bookmarks ~ Seed Awareness—create mosaics with a variety of seeds ~ Mixed herb bouquets and a world map are props for an aromatic look at how herbs have traveled

ABOVE LEFT *Using a magnifier, a Shoot gets a bug's eye view.*
ABOVE RIGHT *A student's patch made for the scarecrow's shirt in the Roots & Shoots garden.*

COOKING with
ROOTS & SHOOTS

LAVENDER LEMONADE

(From the garden: Lemons & Lavender flowers)

1 heaping tablespoon dried lavender flowers
6 lemons
¼ cup sugar (if desired, add more by tablespoons,
   to taste)
Pour 1 cup boiling water over lavender flowers.
Cover and let steep for half an hour.
Meanwhile squeeze lemons, mix with sugar to taste
   (it will be very strong).
Add at least 3 cups cold water.
Strain lavender tea into the lemonade.
Refrigerate.
To serve, pour over ice cubes. Makes 3-6 cups.

DIPPING SAUCE for
RAW APPLES, PEARS, PEACHES,
BERRIES, MELONS, and MORE

*(From the garden: Fresh dipping fruit,
lemon, mint, and honey)*

1 cup plain yogurt
1 tablespoon honey
A squeeze of lemon
Add minced mint leaves or
   cinnamon to taste.
Dip fruit in sauce or mix fruit
   into sauce.
Makes 1 cup.

PUMPKIN MUFFINS

(From the garden: Pumpkin)

1 cup cooked baking pumpkin
   (or canned)
1 cup honey
½ cup vegetable oil
2 eggs
2 cups flour
1 teaspoon baking soda
½ teaspoon salt
½ teaspoon cinnamon
½ teaspoon ginger
½ cup water
½ cup raisins or dried cranberries

Preheat oven to 350 degrees. Combine pumpkin, honey, oil, eggs. Mix well. Mix in flour, baking soda, salt, and spices. Stir in water and raisins (or dried cranberries). Pour into loaf pan or muffin tins. (Use paper liners in tins for easy removal of muffins.) Baking time: mini-muffins 10-15 minutes, regular muffins 20 minutes, loaf 65-75 minutes. Makes approximately 12 regular muffins or 18-24 mini-muffins.

MINT COOKIES

(From the garden: Peppermint leaves)

12 tablespoons unsalted butter
⅔ cup sugar
1 large egg
½ teaspoon vanilla extract

2 cups unbleached, sifted white flour
1 tablespoon minced peppermint leaves
a pinch of salt

Cream butter and sugar. Beat in egg and extract. Gradually mix in the flour. Stir in the minced peppermint and salt. The dough will be soft. Divide dough into 3 parts. Using plastic wrap to shape the dough, roll each part into a cylinder approximately 1¼" in diameter. Chill rolls 1-2 hours.

Preheat oven to 350 degrees. Remove plastic wrap from dough. Slice dough into ¼" thick rounds. Bake on ungreased baking sheet for approximately 10 minutes. Makes approximately 4 dozen cookies.

ABOVE AND OPPOSITE *Pumpkins, lavender, and apples grown and harvested at Gamble.*

Roots & Shoots receives wide recognition beyond the community. Some of its numerous awards include a Youth Garden grant from the National Gardening Association. It was also named one of the top ten Youth Gardens in the United States by the National Garden Association. The program received the prestigious Green Medal Award and was the topic of an invited presentation at the Children's Garden Symposium at the Brooklyn Botanic Garden. Roots & Shoots has been the subject of articles in magazines and featured on local, national, and Canadian television.

ABOVE *A bee condominium in the Roots & Shoots garden welcomes native bees, ones not inclined to sting.* RIGHT *A student-made scarecrow keeping watch over their garden plots discourages plant-raiding critters and enchants people of all ages. This is one from a line of ancestor scarecrows from over the years.* OPPOSITE *Roots & Shoots at work and play at Gamble.*

End-of-Year Party &
Garden Stories

As a child, I thought grandmothers grew in gardens. They were always out there in their old cardigan sweaters, watering the flowers.

—ANNE RAVER

At the end-of-year party, garden stories are shared while everyone enjoys strawberry shortcake and lavender lemonade. Lasting friendships develop among the students and their mentors. They have much to offer each other in their learning… and growing.

THE
CARRIAGE HOUSE
and PATIOS

VENUES FOR CLASSES AND EVENTS

We are convinced by things that show internal complexity, that show the traces of an interesting evolution . . . This is what makes old buildings interesting . . .

—BRIAN ENO

 In its 1902 beginning, the Carriage House was the place for horse-drawn carriages and wagons. Nine years later it became the garage for the Gambles' first car. It was another seventy-five years until an even bigger change came about, when renovations transformed the building into a center for Gamble-sponsored classes and activities and a sought-after setting for private events.

OPPOSITE *The annual Holiday Greens Sale takes place on the patios and offers fresh-cut garden materials for all who deck their halls. A patron finds traditional evergreens, pine, holly, along with boxwood and magnolia, and miniature crabapple branches.*

Another modernization is the full-sized kitchen used for cooking classes and by caterers. An architecturally compatible addition is decorated with hand-painted murals in garden themes. The bank of French doors connects the Carriage House interior to the patios and gardens.

The Carriage House brick patio extends to join with the Tea House Patio nearby, an area partially enclosed by fences and lush planting. With a long season of fair weather, the patios are a favorite for Gamble's receptions, weddings, meetings, and other occasions.

ABOVE *The Carriage House in late spring. In its horse and carriage era, the second story window was an access to the hayloft.*

GARDEN WEDDINGS at GAMBLE

TOP LEFT *Bride and groom looking happily ever after.*
TOP RIGHT *A beaming bride relaxes on a bench.*
BOTTOM *A wedding reception is set up in the Wisteria Garden.*

CLASSES at GAMBLE GARDEN ~ the EDUCATION PROGRAM

The garden is a dynamic universe for exploring, experimenting, and learning. In its mission to provide "a community resource for horticultural education, inspiration, and enjoyment" Gamble sponsors numerous garden-based classes each year. The topics range from garden materials and techniques, to design, cooking, and arts and crafts. All are open to the public at modest fees, and class offerings are different every year. Here are examples of the kinds of classes held at Gamble.

In the Garden

~ CREATING AN HERBAL TEA GARDEN Grow culinary and medicinal herbs to create homemade teas

~ SOFTENING YOUR IDEAS ON HARDSCAPE Elements best for your site; Sculpted earth, paving, structures, and enclosures

~ WAKING UP YOUR GARDEN Spring maintenance, fertilizing, pruning, planting, composting, irrigation inspection

~ GOT CURB APPEAL? Design for a picture-perfect front yard and an inviting entry

~ COMMON SENSE PEST CONTROL Environmentally friendly solutions

~ CREATING AN ENGLISH GARDEN WITH CALIFORNIA NATIVES Comparable effects with drought-tolerant native annuals, perennials, and shrubs

~ GERANIACEAE SMORGASBORD: NEW BLUE GERANIUMS AND ANGEL PELARGONIUMS Advances in hybridizing; Colors from palest sky blue to deep midnight purple; Angel Pelargoniums—compact, long-growing, low maintenance, and 120 selections

ABOVE *Refreshments for a reception following a Gamble class with flowers from the cutting garden.*

For Children & Parents

~ LITTLE SHOP OF HORRORS: CARNIVOROUS PLANTS Identify and cultivate these fascinating plants; How they trap and digest their victims

~ TWILIGHT STORY TIME FOR YOUNG CHILDREN Songs and stories about gardens and growing things; In the Rose Garden

~ DECORATING PAPER Using items from nature, techniques include stamping with fruit and sponging; Ways of using decorated papers

Garden Arts & Inspirations

~ "THE CHANGING GARDEN: FOUR CENTURIES OF EUROPEAN AND AMERICAN ART" Exhibition and Lecture at Stanford University Cantor Center for the Visual Arts, followed by Twilight Supper at Gamble Garden

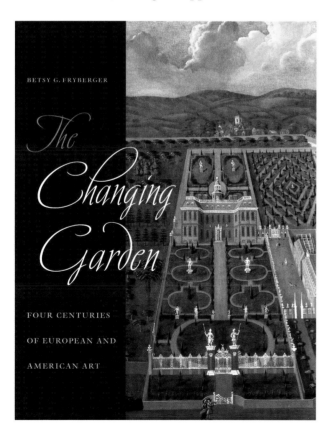

~ OUTSIDE THE BUNGALOW: AMERICA'S ARTS & CRAFTS GARDEN Gates, fencing, walls, paths, water features, and outdoor furniture

~ APPLYING COLOR THEORY IN THE GARDEN Colors and combinations create excitement or serenity; How we respond to colors; Choose annuals and perennials, and plan for color that lasts through the year

~ TREASURES OF BOTANICAL ART Plants and their depiction over the centuries; Man's evolving relationship to the plant world and printmaking techniques

~ FENG SHUI IN THE GARDEN Ancient Chinese principles of placement and design and how to apply them to your garden

ABOVE *The book for the exhibition 'The Changing Garden: Four Centuries of European and American Art.'*

~ GARDEN PHOTOGRAPHY WORKSHOP Two days to photograph and explore different approaches; Find the best view, manage the light, compose and frame pictures

~ THE EVOLUTION OF THE GARDENS AT STANFORD UNIVERSITY MEDICAL CENTER The spectacular results of two decades of gardens that create beautiful and contemplative spaces for patients, their families, and hospital staff within the demands of an industrial building complex

~ LOTUSLAND: THE EXPRESSION OF GANNA WALSKA'S LIFE Photographic tour of this Santa Barbara garden; Forty years in the making, one of the world's most unusual gardens celebrated for its plant collection, water gardens, dramatic setting, and eclectic style

Cooking in the Gamble Kitchen

~ THE LURE OF LAVENDER Cultivating, harvesting, and cooking one of the oldest and most versatile herbs

~ SUMMER SALADS AND SORBETS Festive entrée salads: Chicken and Avocado with Ginger-Mango Vinaigrette, Smoked Salmon and Chevre, Asian Noodle and Grape; Lavender Bread Wreaths. Fruit Sorbets: Mango, Raspberry, and Orange-Pistachio

~ SANTA CRUZ MOUNTAIN WINE TASTING Effects of climate and growing conditions; Blind tasting of fine wines with hors d'oeuvres

~ CHOCOLATE COOKING FÊTE Prepare and sample Spinach Salad with Chocolate Nibs, Salmon Dijon, Quinoa with Cocoa, Chocolate Lava Cakes, and Gelatos

ABOVE *Spring in a garden area at Stanford University Medical Center, subject of a Gamble class.*
OPPOSITE *A shady birdbath area is adjacent to the Carriage House, seen here in autumn. Plants include Japanese maples, rhododendrons, and under planting of ferns, wild ginger, and blue-eyed mary.*

THE
PLEASURE of YOUR
COMPANY

SHARING GARDEN-FRESH FLOWERS AND FOOD

What is pleasanter than the tie of host and guest?

—AESCHYLUS

Garden-fresh flowers and produce inspire hospitality and are central to entertaining in every season and for all occasions. Gamble parties and receptions feature culinary creations that delight both the palate and the eye. Tables and mantels inside the house are graced with fresh-cut flowers from Gamble's garden. Luncheons and receptions, open to the public, always include bounty from the garden. Informally, visitors and Gamble volunteers bring picnics to enjoy at the grand oak area tables and other fresh-air locations.

OPPOSITE *A welcoming bouquet on the front porch of the Gamble Garden house.*

FLOWERS from the CUTTING GARDEN

From early spring and well into autumn, flowers blooming in the Gamble cutting garden are spectacular and worthy of frequent visits to enjoy the ever-changing display. Each year, new perennials and annuals are introduced, where they join the familiar favorites. Gamble's floral designers are well supplied to create weekly fresh arrangements for the house.

TOP *A Gamble volunteer, a professional nurseryman,*
designs and maintains the cutting garden.
BOTTOM *Members of a Bay Area garden club enjoy a*
mid-summer tour of the cutting garden.

The large cutting garden was a favorite of Miss Gamble's who was widely known and appreciated for sharing her flowers. Her floral generosity is echoed today through a joint venture by Gamble with the Garden Club of Palo Alto's outreach program. Gamble provides the flowers for club members to

create and deliver fresh arrangements throughout the community. Delighted and surprised recipients include city agencies, police and fire stations, nursing homes, hospitals, medical clinics, libraries, and schools. As part of some fundraising events, people are invited to bring their own containers for custom arrangements done by Gamble's floral designers using flowers and greens from Gamble.

ABOVE LEFT   *Late summer zinnias are perfect for fresh arrangements.*
ABOVE RIGHT   *Arrangements for outreach are made on the picnic tables in the shade of the oak tree.*

PREPARING FLOWERS
for ARRANGEMENTS

Conditioning

For traditional flower arranging, these techniques for conditioning and preserving flowers will help them last their longest.

Thoroughly water flowers a half-day before cutting. Cut in early morning or after sunset, at least eight hours before arranging.

Take a pail of water to the garden and plunge flower stems in immediately after cutting. Cut on a slant to allow more water to be absorbed.

All flowers and foliage benefit from a long drink—day long or overnight is best. Place flowers in a deep bucket almost filled with tepid water to help them last as long as possible in an arrangement.

Cutting again at a slant, re-cut flower stems under water. Strip leaves from stems that will be below the water line in the arrangement.

Add cool water to arrangements every day. Flowers drink the most in the first six hours after arranging. If a flower head is droopy, re-cut the stem under water.

ABOVE *A centerpiece for a Gamble event includes hydrangeas, roses, calla lilies, and lisianthus.* OPPOSITE, FROM THE TOP *Breadbox poppy, hellebore, sunflower, and eryngium—with industrious bees.*

OPENING WOODY OR BROWN STEMS

For more efficient uptake of water, either hammer end to split, or split with scissors. Strip stem, and if there's new growth, condition in hot water.

Especially good for most foliage plants such as beech, camellia, laurel, lilac, maple, cedar, pine, pieris, loquat, rhododendron, viburnum, wisteria, photinia, pittosporum

SINGEING MILKY STEMS

To seal an oozing stem, singe the cut end with a flame. Put in cold water for several hours.

Especially good for euphorbia, ferns, milkweed, Iceland poppy, peony

FILLING HOLLOW STEMS

This is an old-fashioned treatment that works to help arrangements last well. Hold stem upside down and carefully pour in water; when stem is full, plug end with a small piece of wet cotton—or hold finger tightly over end—place into vase of water.

Especially good for amaryllis, delphinium, lupine

PLUNGING STEMS IN HOT WATER

Pour hot water into container. Protect flowers from the steam to revive wilting plant material, especially sunflowers.

STRAIGHTENING BENDY STEMS

Cut ends, wrap 4-5 flowers in newspaper, secure with string or tape, and place in bucket of water. Leave in cool place overnight.

PRICKING STEMS

Prick with a needle just under flower heads to prevent air bubbles and improve uptake of water for long-lasting arrangements.

Especially good for tulips, hellebores, primulas

ACACIA Peel the cut end 2-3 inches. Add a few drops of gin or vodka to conditioning water.

ALLIUM Place in cool water 6-8 hours; a few drops of Clorox in vase water eliminates onion odor.

ASTER Add one teaspoon of sugar to conditioning water.

BAMBOO Drill a hole down the center of stem to bottom node and fill with water. For smaller stems, place in boiling vinegar 4-5 minutes and submerge in solution of 1 teaspoon salt to 1 quart water for 1 hour. Harden in deep water.

BELLS OF IRELAND Re-cut stem 2 inches from base, split stem, and sink up to its lowest blooms in lukewarm water.

CALLA LILIES Cut stems under water. Add a few drops of gin or vodka to conditioning water.

CYMBIDIUM Cut spike stem ends under water at an angle, 2 inches from base; slit stem 2 inches from bottom. Place in warm water.

DAFFODIL The exuded substance harms other flowers. Allow them to stand alone in water at least 6 hours after cutting and do not re-cut; or, put a few drops of chlorine in vase water.

DAHLIA Char, or dip stems in boiling water; then in cold water up to flower heads overnight.

FERN Submerge in cold water overnight—works for slightly wilted ferns as well.

TOP RIGHT *Daffodil 'Mount Hood'*
BOTTOM LEFT *Dahlia 'Park Princess'*

FREESIA   Condition in water up to flower heads. Keep at 45-50 degrees before arranging.

GARDENIA   Secure tissue paper over bowl with elastic band. Make small holes in paper and push stems through keeping petals out of water.

GLADIOLUS   Cut in middle of the day. Condition at room temperature in 5 tablespoons vinegar to 1 quart water.

GRASSES   Dip stem ends in vinegar for a few minutes; let stand in water, overnight if possible.

HYDRANGEA Hold stem ends in boiling vinegar for 30 seconds, or sear ends in flame. Place immediately into water to condition.

LARKSPUR   Condition 1 hour with ½ teaspoon gin or vodka added to 2 quarts water.

LILAC Cut when blossoms partly open and remove low foliage. Peel bark from base of stem and split. Saturate in a warm preservative solution.

LILY Cut stems under water. Remove stamens to prevent staining and to slow opening process. Condition at least 4 hours.

MOCK ORANGE Cut and put into water with a few drops of added gin or vodka.

NANDINA   Char ends of stems and soak in water 1 hour. Add small amount of salt to the container.

PEONY   Cut when blooms less than half open; hold stem ends in hot salt-water solution for 5 minutes.

TOP LEFT   *Hydrangea macrophylla*
BOTTOM RIGHT   *Peony*

RANUNCULUS Cut when ¾ open. Condition in boiling water before long drink.

ROSE Dip stems in boiling or hot water, then place in tepid or cold up to necks overnight. Remove most leaves and cut stems under water at each stage.

SNAPDRAGON Cut when about half open. Condition in hot water.

SPRING FLOWERING BRANCHES Pick at bud stage, split and scrape stems, put in tepid water to force blooms.

STOCK Condition in very cold water. Strip all foliage below water level. Change water daily.

SWEET PEA Add a few drops of gin or vodka to conditioning water.

TULIP Cut at bud stage. Add a little gin or vodka to conditioning water.

VIOLET Submerge in cold water for 1 hour. A cold water fine mist helps keep them fresh.

WISTERIA Spray blooms and leaves with fine cold water mist. Split woody stems.

ZINNIA Cut when fully open. Remove foliage. Dip stem tips in boiling water.

TOP *Tulip 'Daydream'*
BOTTOM *Zinnia elegans*

Flowers and food are the mainstays of receptions, luncheons, and boutiques that take place in the Gamble House public rooms, where the nearby kitchen and staff offices are abuzz. Other days are inviting times to use the non-circulating Horticultural Reference Library and to take in the architectural features and ambience of the house.

TOP *The library leads to the back porch and Wisteria Garden.* RIGHT *A ceiling light fixture, original to the house, in the living room alcove.*

FROM GARDEN to TABLE

The garden at Gamble is primarily ornamental, feeding the eye and spirit. Inspiration for garden-fresh eating is also at hand, informed by the garden's collection of fruit trees and the extensive Roots & Shoots intergenerational planting beds, which are largely culinary.

Cooking classes at Gamble feature seasonal garden offerings and are popular in the educational program. Fresh produce is a highlight of the luncheons and receptions prepared and served by Gamble volunteers.

Local farmers' markets, increasingly more available, provide quality produce and uncommon choices to expand our eating experience. "From garden to table" encourages us to explore the endless ways to enjoy vegetables, fruits, berries, nuts, herbs, and of course, edible flowers.

ABOVE AND NEXT TWO PAGES *Photographs taken at the farmers' markets in Palo Alto.*

Salad Artistry

Color, texture, proportion, and composition are characteristic of the most appealing salads. Making a salad with these art elements in mind heightens the senses, makes the experience creative, and results in healthy, delicious eating. Start by gathering fresh ingredients from your own garden or local farmers' market. When shopping at a grocery store, choose one with the highest quality seasonal and organic produce.

As you assemble, make a bouquet in your hand or basket to see the emerging color palette. If it needs more variety or brightening, add seasonal splashes such as radishes, beets, cranberries, purple cauliflower, red grapefruit, edible flowers, and orange bell pepper. Seasonal selections, even in winter, lead us to try new ingredients and create more interesting combinations.

Salad making is an opportunity to create freely, outside the confines of strict recipes. Improvise with a seasonal selection of surprise ingredients or unexpected combinations of fruits and vegetables. To please the palate and the eye, add more of what you love most and what is abundantly available; and season to taste.

As main courses or as accompaniments, either tossed or composed, salads bring delectable garden-fresh flavors to any meal. Serve with artisanal breads, bruschetta, grilled panini, or soup. For heartier fare, add chilled or warm thin-sliced lean steak or chicken.

It's incredible how many flowers or parts of flowers I've eaten in the past few years—lavender petals made into ice cream, zucchini blossoms stuffed with ricotta cheese, roses used in butter, to name just a few.

—ROSALIND CREASY

SWEET SURRENDER

The alchemy of baking calls for well-honed recipes. At Gamble-sponsored events, favorite desserts are enlivened with fresh fruit and herbs as both ingredients and eye-catching garnishes. Edible flowers add garden color and lightness to even the richest offerings. These recipes are a sampling of the kind enjoyed at Gamble gatherings.

Zesty Polenta Cake

2 teaspoons grated lemon zest
1 tablespoon grated orange zest
2 ⅔ cups confectioners sugar
1 ½ cups flour
½ cup polenta (coarse ground)
1 ½ teaspoons baking powder
¼ teaspoon salt
4 extra large eggs
⅞ cup olive oil
2 tablespoons Demerara or raw sugar

Preheat oven to 350 degrees. Line a 9-inch spring-form pan with parchment paper and grease side of pan. In a bowl, use a spoon to mash together lemon and orange zests with 1 teaspoon sugar. Using an electric mixer, combine sugar, flour, polenta, baking powder, and salt. Add eggs, one at a time, and beat well on medium speed. Add citrus zest mixture. Slowly pour in the oil, beating until smooth. Beat 1 minute longer and scrape sides of the bowl. Spread batter into prepared pan and sprinkle with Demerara or raw sugar. Once baked, the sugar creates a delightful crunch.

Bake 45-50 minutes, or until toothpick inserted in the center comes out clean. Do not over bake. Allow to cool for 15-20 minutes before removing from pan. Makes 12 servings.

ABOVE *Blossoms on Gamble's Washington navel orange tree.*

Lavender Honey Ice Cream

    2 tablespoons lavender flowers, fresh or dried
    2 cups half-and-half or milk
    2 eggs
    2 egg yolks
    ⅔ cup honey
    1 cup whipping cream

In the top of a double boiler, heat the lavender and half-and-half, or milk, until steaming. Let cool slightly and press through a sieve, discarding lavender. Whisk the eggs and yolks until blended and beat in the honey. Whisk in some of the hot half-and-half, return to the pan, and cook over hot water, stirring constantly, until the custard coats the spoon. Immediately place in a pan of cold water and stir the custard while letting it cool. Pour into a container, cover and chill thoroughly. When you are ready to freeze the mixture, stir in the cream. Freeze according to the directions for your ice cream maker. Makes 1 quart.

Lemon Thyme Madeleines

    ¼ lb. butter, melted and cooled
    4 eggs
    ¼ teaspoon salt
    ⅔ cup sugar
    zest of one lemon
    1 teaspoon lemon extract
    1 teaspoon dried thyme
    ¾ cup sifted flour
    ¼ cup corn meal

Preheat oven to 350 degrees. Beat eggs, salt, and sugar together until thick, about 8 minutes. Fold in flour and corn meal. Add lemon extract, butter, thyme, and lemon zest. Spoon mixture into buttered Madeleine pans. Bake until golden, about 10-12 minutes. Remove from pans and cool on racks. Makes 2 dozen.

ABOVE *Lavender and lemons growing in Gamble's garden.*

Nuts-About-Pumpkin Cookies

½ cup butter
1 cup dark brown sugar, firmly packed
1 egg
⅔ cup pumpkin puree
1 teaspoon vanilla extract
1 ½ cup all-purpose flour
½ teaspoon baking powder
1 teaspoon baking soda
1 teaspoon ground cinnamon
1 teaspoon nutmeg
½ teaspoon ground cloves
1 ½ cup dried cranberries
1 ½ cup walnut halves
1 tablespoon orange zest

Preheat oven to 350 degrees. Lightly grease 2 baking sheets, or line with parchment paper.

Spread walnuts on a small baking pan and bake until lightly toasted, 8-10 minutes. Break or chop into smaller pieces.

In large bowl, beat butter until creamy. Mix in brown sugar. Beat until fluffy. Add egg, pumpkin, vanilla, and orange zest. Beat until blended.

In another bowl, stir together flour, baking powder, baking soda, cinnamon, nutmeg, and cloves. Add dry ingredients to pumpkin mixture. Mix until incorporated. Stir in cranberries and walnuts. Drop rounded teaspoons onto prepared baking sheets.

Bake 13-15 minutes, until golden brown. Longer baking time results in crunchier cookies. Transfer cookies to wire racks to cool. Store in airtight container for 3-4 days, or freeze.

Makes 4 dozen cookies.

ABOVE *Pumpkin patch harvest at Gamble Garden.*

COMMUNITY DAY

CELEBRATING AUTUMN

*The universe is a continuous web.
Touch it at any point and the whole web quivers.*

—STANLEY KUNITZ

Deep blue skies, the altered slant of sunlight, and crisp cool nights signal autumn and, for Gamble Garden, Community Day. It is a day of garden pleasures to herald the new season with its shift from summer's floral extravagance to the rich color palette of pumpkins, squashes, and changing leaves.

OPPOSITE *The Black Tupelo (Nyssa sylvatica) trees
—along the Churchill Avenue and the Waverley Street
boundaries of Gamble—turn brilliant crimson in fall.*

On Community Day, earthworms are stocked in an unplanted area of the garden set aside for the earthworm digging contest. Children are provided with trowels in this heated competition to find the longest earthworm. After careful measuring, the length of each challenger earthworm is recorded alongside the name of its discoverer.

ALL PHOTOS *Young diggers search for wigglers.*

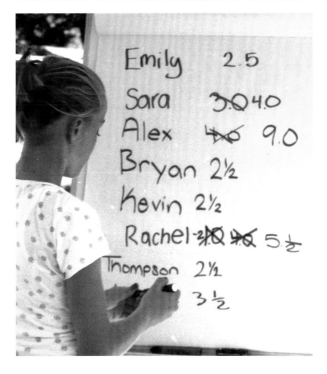

Emily   2.5
Sara   ~~3.0~~ 4.0
Alex   ~~4.0~~ 9.0
Bryan   2½
Kevin   2½
Rachel ~~3.0~~ ~~4.0~~ 5½
Thompson 2½
            3½

There is no limit to how many entries one can offer up in attempts to best the current leader, and after hours of digging, a winner is announced. The earthworms, spent from the experience, are returned to the well-aerated soil.

TOP LEFT AND RIGHT *Each earthworm is carefully measured.* BOTTOM LEFT *Records are kept to determine the winner in the earthworm digging contest.*

ABOVE *Budding designers create bouquets at the children's flower worktable.*
OPPOSITE *Toddler meets succulents.*

Activities, services, and displays are set up throughout the garden. A boutique features homemade jams and baked goods, pumpkins, and seasonal decorations that celebrate nature's bounty. Plant sales are brisk for advantageous fall planting. Many of the sought-after plants for purchase have been propagated in the Gamble Greenhouse.

Fresh-cut flowers from Gamble and containers for bouquets draw scores of children to make their own mini-arrangements to take home. Each year favorite activities return and new ones are introduced. Expert tool sharpening is available, demonstrations are offered—in beekeeping for example—and vintage farm equipment and garden tools are displayed.

Salvia greggii 'Moonlight'/S. x jamensis Autumn Sage

$8⁰⁰

Grown By Gamble Garden Volunteers

Autumn sage is a native of southwest Texas and the deserts of Mexico. It is closely related to Salvia microphylla, which it resembles and with which it readily hybridizes. It flowers throughout summer and autumn with a wide range of flower colors (mostly red shades in the wild). Plant in well-drained soil where plant will be in the sun for most of the day. Prune back dead wood and shape the plant before new growth appears in spring.

'Moonlight' is a hybrid of S. greggii or of S. greggii and S. microphylla (S. x jamensis). It has pale yellow flowers. It grows to about 3' tall and wide.

Salvia chionophylla

$8⁰⁰

Grown By Gamble Garden Volunteers

Salvia chionophylla comes from a small area in the Coahuila province of Mexico, but has proven highly adaptable to garden use. It is a gray-leaved prostrate plant that roots as it grows along the ground, lightly covering a large area, but can be trained to a more compact habit by pruning the trailing growth. It looks lovely trailing over the edge of a container. Blue flowers appear from early summer through autumn. Provide full sun, well drained soil and regular water.

TOP *Mini-pumpkins planted with violas are for sale at the boutique.* BOTTOM *For the plant sale, flyers give information for the gardener and show the plant in its mature stage.*

Live music fills the air, and voices of all ages enthusiastically follow the Sing-a-long Man. He knows all the favorite tunes and has new ones to teach.

The Butterfly Man's display is set up in the shade of the grand oak area, where his stories draw a big crowd. Little hands are busy working on a variety of craft projects, making leaf prints, and fashioning dolls from dried cornhusks. Children climb up on hay bales for tractor rides to enjoy life in the slow lane.

TOP LEFT *The Sing-a-long Man brings his guitar and song charts.* TOP RIGHT *Morris dancers entertain.* BOTTOM RIGHT *Crafts with autumn leaves.*

Elizabeth F. Gamble Garden

A COMMUNITY HORTICULTURAL FOUNDATION

Open to the public during daylight hours

Explore Gamble Garden!

See how many of the garden features shown in the photographs you can find.

Where is it?

Parking

Carriage House

Rose Garden

Allée

Rest Rooms

Greenhouse

Horticulturist Office

Wisteria Garden

Gamble House

Tea House

Roots & Shoots

Gazebo

Parking

Elizabeth F. Gamble Garden

TOP *On Community Day longtime Gamble volunteers generously loan Henry, their beautifully maintained, fully operational 1935 Ford pickup truck.* RIGHT *Interior tours to inspect Henry's vintage features are welcomed.* OPPOSITE *An exploration map especially for children to lead adults around Gamble and locate garden features.*

The moment one gives close attention to anything, even a blade of grass, it becomes a mysterious, awesome, indescribably magnificent world in itself.

—HENRY MILLER

ABOVE *In the middle of all the activity, a child finds a quiet moment to peer into the butterfly specimen cases and books.*
OPPOSITE *A small visitor engaged in fashioning a bouquet to take home.*

ABOVE *Two of Miss Gamble's favorites, irises and chocolate cake, in a Gamble volunteer's own garden — a garden that has been on Spring Tour.*

After she had passed the milestone of her ninetieth birthday,

Harriet Morse, author of Gardening in the Shade,

shared her secret of a long life filled with health and happiness:

"I look at every person I encounter and say or think

with all my might, 'I wish you well.' "

Photography and Art Credits

Cover and Opening Pages

Front dust jacket photo by John Stocklin
Gazebo in cover photo designed by Bob Waterman, Waterman & Sun, Palo Alto
End papers and cover drawing by John Haynes
Jane Stocklin: ii
Susan Woodman: v / x / xii
Joanne Koltnow: ix

Gamble Now and Then   pp. 14 - 27

Susan Woodman: 14 / 17 above right / 18 / 22/ 23 / 25 / 26 top right
John Stocklin: 15 / 21 / 24
Gamble Garden archives: 16 / 17 above left / 19 / 20
p. 18: Mural in photo painted by Leslie McLaren
Poster of Gamble Garden on easel from a painting by Brent Jensen
Merrill Jensen: 26 bottom left
Susan Benton: 27

New Pathways in an Old Garden   pp. 28 - 51

Merrill Jensen: 28 / 29 / 34 / 39 / 41 center / 43 top / 44 / 49 right / 51
pgs. 30-31: Garden plan drawing by Nancy Singer for Gamble Garden
John Stocklin: 32 / 42 top / 46 / 47
Doug Woodman: 33 top
Susan Benton: 33 bottom / 35 top / 41 top & bottom / 43 right / 50 top left
Jane Stocklin: 35 bottom
Susan Woodman: 36 / 37 / 38 / 40 / 42 right / 45 / 48 / 49 top / 50 bottom left & bottom right

Tending and Groundskeeping   pp. 52 - 59

Susan Woodman: 52 / 54 top right / 55 top right & bottom left / 56 top left / 58 top
Merrill Jensen: 53 / 55 top left / 56 bottom left / 57 above left / 58 / 59 bottom left
Jane Stocklin: 54 bottom / 59 top left
Susan Benton: 54 top left / 56 bottom right / 57 above right
Doug Woodman: 59 top right & bottom right

Spring Tour   pp. 60 - 73

Vanessa Roach: 60 far left, top & bottom / 69 bottom right
Susan Woodman: 60 near left, top & bottom / 62 / 64 top left / 66 top right /
        67 top right & bottom right / 69 left / 70 top right / 72 top right / 73
Susan Benton: 60 near left, center / 63 / 64 top right & bottom left / 65 / 66 bottom left /
        67 top left / 68 top left & bottom left / 69 right / 71 / 72 top left & bottom left
Chris Stein: 61 / 68 top right & bottom right
Jane Stocklin: 66 top left
p. 70: bottom left, graphic design by Gary Nusinow for Gamble Garden

Art in the Garden   pp. 74 - 79

Susan Woodman: 74 / 75 / 76 right / 77 / 79 left
Merrill Jensen: 76 top / 79 top
Doug Woodman: 78

Roots & Shoots   pp. 80 - 89

Susan Benton: 80 / 81 / 82 top / 83 / 84 / 85 / 86 / 87 / 89
Susan Woodman: 82 right / 88 above
Gamble Garden archives: 88 right

Carriage House and Patios   pp. 90 - 97

Susan Woodman: 90 / 92 / 94/ 96
Jane Stocklin: 91
p. 93: top left, Norbert von der Groeben, photographer; with permission
p. 93: top right & bottom, Larissa Cleveland, photographer; with permission
Merrill Jensen: 97

The Pleasure of Your Company   pp. 98 - 113

Jane Stocklin: 98 / 103 second from top
Susan Benton: 99 / 101 / 102 / 103 bottom / 104 top right / 106 / 112 right
Susan Woodman: 100 / 103 third from top / 105 bottom right / 107 top / 108 / 109 / 110 / 111 / 112 left
Merrill Jensen: 103 top / 104 bottom left / 105 top left / 113
Bill Stocklin: 107 right

Community Day   pp. 114 - 127

Merrill Jensen: 114 / 115
Susan Benton: 116 top left & bottom right / 117 top right / 118 bottom / 119 / 120 top / 121 / 123
Susan Woodman: 116 top right / 117 top left & bottom left / 124
p. 118 top: photo courtesy of the children's family
Chris Stein: 120 bottom
p. 122: adapted from Gamble Garden Exploration Maps
Joanne Koltnow: 125
Jane Stocklin: 126
End papers drawing by John Haynes
Dust jacket author photo by Doug Woodman
Back dust jacket photo by Susan Woodman

Sources and Permissions

Cover and Opening Pages

p. v   Sir George Sitwell (1860-1943), *On the Making of Gardens* (1909).
p. viii   Dan Kiley (1913-2004) landscape architect, from an interview. Reprinted with permission from the Burlington Free Press, Vermont.

Gamble Now and Then   pp. 14 - 27

p. 15   Robert Dash, in *A Gardener's Bouquet of Quotations*, Maria Polushkin Robbins (Dutton 1993).
p. 18   Stephen C. Gruber, "Gamble landmark: P.A.'s inherited house in disrepair," *Peninsula Times Tribune*, May 7, 1985.
p. 20   Palo Alto Lawn Bowls information from their web site

New Pathways in an Old Garden   pp. 28 - 51

pp. 28-51   Horticultural information: Canopy's Gamble Garden Tree Walk and 'A Walk Through Gamble Garden', a self-guided tour brochure by Betsy Freyberger, Mary McCullough, and Jane Stocklin
p. 29   © Mirabel Osler, A Breath From Elsewhere, (Bloomsbury Publishing Plc. 1999), quoted with permission
p. 34   Thomas Pakenham, *Meetings with Remarkable Trees*, (Random House 1996), quoted with permission.
p. 36   Richard Sheridan (1751-1816), Irish playwright and poet
p. 38   Thomas D. Church, in *A Gardener's Bouquet of Quotations,* Maria Polushkin Robbins (Dutton 1993).
p. 44   By Octavio Paz, translated by Eliot Weinberger, from A TALE OF TWO GARDENS, copyright ©1996 by Octavio Paz and Eliot Weinberger. Reprinted by permission of New Directions Publishing Corp.

p. 47   Eleanor Perenyi, *Green Thoughts*, (Random House 1981); quoted with permission. Tending and
         Groundskeeping   pp. 52 - 59

p. 53   E. B. White, *One Man's Meat* (Harper Colophon 1983).

Spring Tour   pp. 60 - 73

p. 61   William Shakespeare (1564-1616), *A Midsummer-Night's Dream*.

Art in the Garden   pp. 76 - 81

p. 77   Sir Walter Scott (1771-1832) Scottish novelist, playwright, and poet.

Roots & Shoots   pp. 80 - 89

Information from Gamble Garden's Roots & Shoots original and recent curricula

p. 89   Anne Raver, 'Reflections on a Year in the Garden,' L.A. Times-Washington Post News Service, 1986.

Carriage House and Patios   pp. 90 - 97

p. 91   From HOW BUILDINGS LEARN by Stewart Brand, copyright (c) 1994 by Stewart Brand.
         Used by permission of Viking Penguin, a division of Penguin Group (USA) LLC.

p. 95   Book cover art reproduced with permission of the Iris & B. Gerald Cantor Center for Visual
         Arts at Stanford University.

The Pleasure of Your Company   pp. 98 - 113

p. 99   Aeschylus (525-456 BC) Greek playwright

pp. 102-106 'Preparing Flowers for Arrangements' courtesy of Carmen Pekelsma

pp. 111, 112 above, and 113: Lou Pappas, consultant

p. 112 below: recipe courtesy of Carmen Pekelsma

p. 112   Rosalind Creasy, *The Edible Flower Garden* (1999). Used by permission of Tuttle Publishing.

Community Day   pp. 114 - 127

p. 115   From THE WILD BRAID: A POET REFLECTS ON A CENTURY IN THE GARDEN
         by Stanley Kunitz and Genine Lentine. Copyright 2005 by Stanley Kunitz and Genine Lentine.
         Used by permission of W.W. Norton & Company, Inc.

p. 124   quote attributed to Henry Miller

p. 127   quote attributed to Harriet Morse